CW01558844

Rescue Contraptions

poetry

Joe Duggan

tall-lighthouse

Cover Design: Flora Hands, Carline Creative

A CIP record for this book is available
from the British Library

published 2022 by tall-lighthouse

ISBN 978 1 904551 03 4

tall-lighthouse
www.tall-lighthouse.co.uk

for
Michael & Francy

contents

i

Julie Andrews

Da brought home bombs in many sizes
from petrol, to incendiary, to suspect devices,
but the worst of all, unexploded,
sitting on the coffee table
waiting for something to detonate it:
a question, an answer,
too many spuds on the wrong plate.

How the hell did you put up with it?
When you came home from your night shift
you might as well have kept your uniform on all week.
I see you in my memory as Julie Andrews as a nurse,
always on call, for when the bombs went off.

Don't be Vague

"Don't be vague, ask for Haig"
                            Whisky advert

One time he was on the sick
and was called up to The Board.
He didn't want to get taken off
because there was no work.
They sent him into a cubicle to undress.
On the inside door someone had scrawled
DON'T BE VAGUE, KILL A TAIG.

Put my blood pressure through the roof.
I had thon boyos to thank
for another six weeks sick pay.
These are the jokes of my childhood,
the little gifts my da used to survive,
and to feed us.

Castlewellan

Just another day of your coughing
and spluttering,
your systems packing in
and the morphine never quite strong enough
and the pillow never quite soft enough
and never quite the right way
to rest your swollen, reddened feet.

Being County Down,
half the ward knew you
and three quarters of their visitors,
so, when a dour-faced man,
older than you, but much fresher,
gasped *Ach, it's not yourself, is it?*
I welcomed the distraction.

After your pained nod of permission
he sat down and it's the usual:
the cousin of, the brother of, who left the farm to him,
the two of you knitting Castlewellan
fields and lanes over the bed.

I almost doze off
into some back road past Clanvaraghan
that I pretend to know until
What about the horse?
Did Da just chortle?

The fella with the horsebox
was taking too long,
couldn't get the horse to go in,
so your da here just jumps on
and rides the big white mare
from Rostrevor to Castlewellan.

That's where I leave this setting.
I have no desire to recount
the screams, more morphine,
so that's where I leave it,
and place my young father,
lean and upright,
trotting into Castlewellan Square
on his white horse,
the hero, the cowboy, the man.

The Globe

Annsborough School, 1946

There is a story about how my da and
another boy were told to get the globe
from the back of the class but somehow
in teetering towards the front
they let it slip and every child
watched as it flew across the room.

Bryansford Cemetery, 2002

As I watch my da getting lowered in,
Uncle John, in tears, says
You know you were asking
about him breaking the globe?

He nods over at the gravedigger,
clabbered in mud, ready with his spade.
That's the boy that was with him.
Go over and ask.
Standing over the big hole
in our world, we still like a good story.

I hear you were with my da
when youse dropped the globe?
He nods towards the open grave.
We didn't drop it – did he tell you that?
The wee fucker tripped me.

The original line-up

ever since the lower sixth concert,
Wayne McKibben on fender guitar,
Ringo Mooney on drums,
Eamon McKibben on vocals,
Gary Doyle on bass,
and me, who sometimes helped them set up,
especially if a crowd had started to gather.

There was a certain way to carry a guitar
to suggest you knew how to handle and play it.
I became practiced at this.
This was my brief performance.
I wanted to get it right.

A casual *I carry guitars everyday* walk.
A cool *I am in fact part of the band, secretly
write all their songs, and would play
if I wasn't so blasé* walk.

Don't bother me or speak to me.
I am carrying this guitar.
Can't you see I am carrying this guitar?
I also smoke.

Summer in Belfast

Maybe it's getting drunk with Seany in the park,
Budweiser when Budweiser still tasted interesting,
sunny day in Belfast worth a celebration alone.
I was reading a poem about Tuscany. We were
supposed to be studying, not Tuscany,
but all I wanted to read about was Tuscany.
Grapes spill from the wagon, purple-stain the sun.

Seany was half-studying physics, half-studying the talent.
As the sun grew hotter the words began to jumble.
It is summer in Belfast and everyone's burning.
Let us drink from our cans in Botanic Gardens.
Who dares examine us? Who dares to tell us what we
                                        should know?
It is summer in Belfast in Tuscany Gardens.
The sun is purple and Seany's stained with Budweiser.
All the girls are purple and our books are flown away.
Which girl will tell us what we need to know?

The heat is burning my poem about Tuscany.
The heat is burning the page of the Gardens.
The gardener is a centaur who pitchforks the soil.
Let's stay here all night in Tuscany Gardens
and sleep with our new girlfriends near the
                                        Japanese bridge.
I am looking back with confidence from thirty years later.
I've got the lines now. I'll whisper them in my ear:
It is summer in Belfast in Botanic Gardens.
Drop your book by the girl in the purple shorts.
Just tell her it's midsummer and soon we will be older.
Tell Seany to get up and set up a party.
Tell Seany you like him because you're not still in touch.
Tell Seany he'll make it, but not what he wanted.
Tell Seany he's alright and a good mate and a mucker
but you might want to leave that until you've had a few
                                        more drinks.

Because it's summer in Belfast and everything's burning.
In Botanic Gardens the fires rise without harming.
In Botanic Gardens the fires are just in your bodies.
You will still be there at midnight, and you will fail the exam.
Your da will kill you but you will pass the resit.
You will graduate with honours, and I still don't know
                                        what that means.
So just sit where you're sitting and enjoy the commotion,
the ice-cream van, the girls playing, the drunks on the bench.
Because it's summer in Belfast in Tuscany Gardens.
At 4 a.m. you will leave, catch your jeans on the fence.

Jim will cut his leg and you will take him to hospital,
but nothing hurt then and you all laughed at the doctors
who asked you to all leave and not come back 'til the morning,
past the twenty-four-hour garage and the dare to buy porn,
past Lisburn Road bakery and the daftness of daybreak.

If I could send you one whisper into your testosterone ear
I'd say: enjoy it and don't worry, enjoy it and don't worry,
you'll crash and you'll burn again every few years,
but those that you're walking with, they turned out alright.

And that includes you, so take summer in Belfast and
                                        scrape your exams,
clean up your room and get back your deposit,
you've got more nights to go walking,
sometimes in company, but often alone.

The Lucky Bar

I was drinking here the night this bar was particularly lucky.
World Cup '94. Republic of Ireland vs Italy.

Coming to you live from Giants Stadium, New Jersey.
The stands are awash with a sea of green.
This is like a home game, surely, for the Irish.

I don't want to sit beside the window. Why? I just don't. Let
me sit over there. OK. Come on ya boys. Houghton outside
the box. Lovely dip. Italian goalkeeper off the line. Oh Christ
I don't believe it. Fuck. One-Nil. Ireland One, Italy Nil.

Goooooooaaaaaalaccccchio.

Head-beer-spill. Danny is dancing on the table. Teresa is
jiving between the tables, her handbag swinging. Julie and
Sarah have started a conga. 11th minute. Reports are coming
in. Only 79 minutes to hold them off. Pull down the shutters
lads – they're not getting in. *O-laay, O-laay, O-laay, O-laay.*
Pints of Harp and oooh and aaaah but they're not getting
in. Paul McGrath with another header. Boot it up the field.

Ooh-aah Paul McGrath, say Ooh-aah Paul McGrath.
We're all part of Jackie's Army.

Big haymaker clearance from Packie Bonner. Full. Time.
Whistle. We have fucking beaten Italy. Raymy the barman
is clapping on top of a chair.

And we'll really shake them up
When we win the World Cup
'Cause Ireland are the greatest football team.

Rattle on the windows. What the fuck. Benny and a crowd
from Quinns with a huge tricolour draped over their heads.
Laughing. Don't do that. Scared the shit out of us. Raymy
says we can have another round. Reports are coming in.

Teresa is dancing and tottering between the tables. Danny is dancing with her handbag on his head. Danny's da has got up and is dancing with his wife even though the music has stopped. Reports are coming in. Danny grabs his ma and starts swinging her arms. Head-beer-spill. *Whisht.* A pasty-faced Northern Ireland newsreader is haunting the footage from the States. Reports are coming in. *Whisht.* Danny and Teresa are under the big TV.

Newsflash along the bottom of the screen in red and black. Reports are coming in of a shooting in the Heights Bar, County Down. County Down? Several deaths. Where's the Heights bar? Never heard of it. Must be Newry or somewhere. Beer-spill. Sarah comes back from the bar. She doesn't have any drinks. Raymy says the Heights Bar is O'Toole's. Fuck off, if it was O'Toole's it would say O'Toole's. The report said Loughinisland. Ten miles away. Raymy heard it. There's been a phone call. Danny is dancing between the tables. Teresa comes up behind him and whispers in his ear. Their dance slows.

It's not fucking O'Toole's. The Heights Bar is O'Toole's. What about Seany? Sarah's Beezer does the taxis to O'Toole's. Especially at weekends. Sarah starts crying. Danny and Teresa are rocking gently in the corner. Danny's parents are putting on their coats. Raymy whispers to our table that it would be a good idea to leave. He's going round all the tables. There's been a phone call.

We go to the flat. Seany does shifts in O'Toole's. I think about ringing. We try Beezer's taxi number. I talk a lot about Seany. Julie asks why I don't ring my friend but I don't. It's late. I crack open a can. Late-night News. Yellow tape police cordons and ambulances. Number's gone up to six.

Breakfast TV. Local priest and MP on the news. Hangover fry-up, cutlery clanking and quiet talk in the kitchen. Phone rings. Sarah bursts into tears. Beezer is OK. I lie on the sofa staring at Mr Motivator.

A week later, a pint with Seany and Paul. He was away that night. Changed shifts. After some bad jokes from Paul, we shut up and Seany starts talking. Ghost stories. Check the exits. *Whisht.*

The week before it happened, Seany and the other barmen talked about the spate of pub shootings. They speculated on what they would do if gunmen burst in. Seany said he would crouch down and make his way to the back exit. Shorty said he'd run for the toilets and go out that way. Seany argued that would leave him out in the open too long.

I hate this storytelling. Don't tell me the next bit. I'm leaving now lads. I'm off to America. But I don't say any of that and all three of us just sit there sipping on our pints. I have to ask the question. Which way did he go? He went for the toilets and they got him. He's still in hospital but we think he's going to make it.

Other ghost stories swirl around the County Down farms and fields. They know who did it. The same men who did those other shootings. The police knew. Hooded men trying to get into another pub close by, just after the shooting. But someone phoned and shutters went down and everyone froze until the knocking ended. Thin metal, rattling against the quietest, soberest bar in Ireland. Loughinisland, Ballykinlar, they were heading south, they were heading towards us.

This is a lucky bar. With lucky shamrocks on the wall. Check the exits. Glance towards the door.

Even after another builder was shot

Michael still needed the work
so the whole crew agreed
to get back in the van
and drive to Tiger's Bay
winding each other up
the whole way there
where the foreman said one of them
should take turns to look out
for any strange cars slowing down.

On the drive back from Belfast
the craic was good until
he got out and threw up
by the side of the road,
holding himself steady
on the sign for his hometown.

ii

Holy Land Pastorals

i shepherd of Yafi

Slumped in a Nazareth pine forest
sobering up after a lemon vodka
all-nighter to goat bells and *yalla yalla*
from the Arab shepherd who does not
stop to interrogate this parka'd
pretend paramilitary
who's just time-jumped ceasefires.

ii elder in the ruins of Iqrit

*The kibbutz cows have more land
than the Palestinians. This village
was razed to the ground by a force
led by a young soldier you may have
heard of – Yitzhak Rabin?*

But he's just signed the peace deal with Jordan.
I thought he was one of the good guys?
He is.

iii campfire after Yad Vashem

a single hair caught on the twig
curls into a red-meat knot
that crumbles on touch.

iv Tel Aviv techno bar 2am

My grandfather still had the numbers
on his arm. We sang the Kaddish for him
but it was not, how you say, a lament?
We call it *keening* in Ireland.
If anyone tries that again
they will hear this instead.
She pats the Uzi hanging off
her shoulder as we down another shot.

Oscar Wilde at Clapham Junction

*On November 13th, 1895, I was brought down here from
London. From two o'clock till half-past two I had to
stand on the centre platform of Clapham Junction in
convict dress, and handcuffed, for the world to look at.*

De Profundis

Jostled to the front,
a slovenly figure
in weak camouflage of grey,
I pivot between stand and fall.

Who is this beautiful boy,
languid and long in uniform,
striding this way,
no eyes for me?

Another half hour, you say.
Tolerable, until
the first carriage pulls in.

A lady in an ill-fitting hat stares
gormlessly until the penny drops
then clasps her friend's arm
to transmit the news through the train.

A little boy struggles to understand.
His mother hisses in his ear.
His eyes widen at the odious man.

After each train the circle grows.
My toes claw deeper inside my shoes.
Seven trains I greet that day,
an odd ambassador of shame.

You know, the reason why
this is worse than a real death
is that one does not have to *live*
with one's real death.

And the most painful thing
is not to be hung,
but to be *seen* to be hung.

London Prices

In Kensington they tell the Russian
who owns the English football team
that a kitchen is worth two million,
a million alone for the kitchen sink,
and the chorus ripples outwards to the suburbs
What is this worth? What is this worth?

None of us in the stupid jobs can afford ourselves,
the teachers, nurses, poets, but instead take a night in
pacing around our flats, opening cupboard doors
What is this worth? What is this worth?

We go for a walk in Crystal Palace Park
but it's cordoned off by the Clown Mayor
leading around businessmen in suits,
pointing at playgrounds, trees and ponds,
chortling like an estate agent on cocaine
What is this worth? What is this worth?

We go to the shops but are stopped by
an architecture student with a clip board
who wants to know what we would like
to see on the last available piece of green:

    a) a Tesco
    b) an oil rig
    c) an interpretative centre about workhouses
    d) an interpretative centre about our lost parks
       OR
    e) a mixed-use residential block including at
       least one affordable flat (for the caretaker)

I ask her about libraries or hospitals
or maybe even planting a few more trees
but she gives me a quizzical look and says
there's no box for that and anyway
what is that worth?

We take a day by the sea but all the way down
we survey small houses in nice villages with good shops
so that the earworm rings as our Instagram kerchings
at the pebbles, the sky, the burnt-out pier.

We can't afford ourselves here either,
the builders, the nurses, all the poets
who can't afford to stop for adjectives
but instead are condemned to end
every verse of our rushed lives
with the repeating chorus
What is this worth? What is this worth?

Teacher Training

i The New Criteria

By the end of this lesson, your class must be able to make clear cross-curricular links.

Your classroom environment must reflect current learning, and mounted displays must rotate seven times within the course of the lesson.

By the end of this lesson, the children from the estate must attain admission to Oxbridge.

During the lesson, it must become evident that the children's brains have increased in size, and all children from all groups must attain at least one major superpower that reflects their ethnic background and gender.

During the lesson, we will need to observe the children's skin colour turn more agreeable and their accent tune into Radio 4.

By the end of this lesson, the teaching must demonstrate a wide range of technologies, including lasers and small nuclear warheads.

This lesson will be assessed against the criteria set for the Olympics Opening Ceremony, but with no additional budget.

During this lesson, the children must burst into tongues, split the atom, and solve the Middle East question without the use of a calculator.

By the end of this lesson, you must must must must must must always outstanding must...

By the end of this lesson, the children must recapture the British Empire.

By the end of this lesson, if you are still alive you will be marked inadequate.

ii The New Objective

In our war against Islam
my mission seems to be
getting Abdi, Salaman
and Mohammed
up to Level 4 in maths.

I think Abdi and Salaman might make it.
I'm not so sure about Mohammed
but then it is dangerous
to have preconceived ideas
about people.

In our war against Islam
the suspects at assembly
seem to have forgotten their weapons
but instead laugh at my jokes,
put their hands up with good ideas,
and seem more bothered about
whether or not they will be allowed
to play football on the ball court
than destroying me and my
righteous Western values.

In our war against Islam
I finally smash through the
conspiracy of silence around
what happens in the mosque
by asking Mariam in Year 2
to come up off the carpet
to do a *show and tell* about it.

Look Up, East Sheen

To be surrounded on all sides by cloud.
To be surrounded on all sides by sound.
To be light. As the temperature drops
I begin to think Europe is very cold.

The runway at Luanda airport was badly
lit and badly guarded. At 5.30 a.m.
I slipped through the fence.
Curled up against the wheel
I knew something wasn't right.

Zooming in on the Google map,
zooming in, with no option to zoom out.
Surrounded on all sides by cloud.
surrounded on all sides by sound.
To be light.

The coroner will say I lost consciousness
before the fall. I think I can see Big Ben.
I think I can see the snake of the Thames,
the beautiful gardens of the suburbs,
the golf course on the other bank.

The coroner will say I have already passed out
from hypothermia. The coroner will say my injuries
are consistent with a fall from a great height.
The airport authorities will express concerns
about security.

My name is Youssop Matada.
Although I was buried in Twickenham,
I am still surrounded by air.
I can still see the snake of the Thames,
the beautiful gardens of the suburbs,
the golf course on the other bank.

Look up, fellow citizens of East Sheen.
I will come falling at high speed
each year on my birthday.
I will come falling to a pavement near you,
with a single English pound in my pocket,
and a sightseer's map in my head.

Look up.

Robbie's Phone
i.m. R.G.

It was a spot on the map,
last signal on his phone,
for the first nine days
that was all that was known.

Despite all the sightings
and Facebook call-outs,
all we knew was that he
got to that point and then
either his battery died
or he turned it off.
Could have been stolen.
He turned us all into detectives.

For a man who spent his time
tweeting and sharing
the joy of this town,
supporting and liking,
cheering things on,
who used his phone to
photograph and amplify,
campaign to keep the library open,
community gardens, markets, gigs,
anything that was live, to know
he'd got to that point and then
either his battery died
or he turned it off.
It was early in the day
for his battery to die.

iii

Francy

The bell rings, and he comes out punching for the 47th round.
The 46th had been tough, but better than the 45th when
he'd lost his mum and spent two months in a strange ward
where he didn't know any of the staff and every shadow
was a threat beyond the average imagination.

And of course he's been in training for years and has
developed many techniques over the previous rounds:
three photocopies of the same Rocky Marciano picture
blu-tacked so he can see him wherever he goes in his flat;
a mental map of all the cafes in Belfast that do free refills
and don't mind if you sit on for a bit; a back catalogue
of classic fights to play during shadow boxing; my number
written on the wall, and a few other family and friends'
who won't give off if he rings too late; affirmations, targets
and goals, all over the walls, targets and goals;

a gallery of ring men, corner men and supporters;
books and DVDs arranged so he can see them cheering
him on, especially when he gets up late on duvet days,
De Niro in *Raging Bull*, Brando *On the Waterfront*,
Pacino and Duvall, Michael Collins, St Anthony, Steve Biko,
Dr Wayne Dyer, Jersey Joe Walcott, Jack Dempsey, Simon
and Garfunkel, Michelle Pfeiffer and Mahatma Gandhi;

a cut-out article about a woman who took up running
in her fifties and lost a load of weight;
anything that can help you get out of bed,
anything that can help you get out the door
on one of those particularly bad duvet days.
When your brain gets scrambled every three years, you've
got to know how to rebuild your world from scratch.

So the bell rings and he comes out fighting for the 47th,
bobbing and weaving, jab, jab, keep up your guard, lead
with the left, targets and goals, targets and goals,
talking about a 5k and signing up for that computer course.

Ladeez and gentlemen! I give you, in the red corner,
fighting out of Burrendale Estate and Belfast,
in the extremely colourful shorts,
the undisputed, undefeated,
heavyweight champion
of my world.

The Admission Procedure
after David Peace

There is a phone call. I go back.
I try to find him. Follow the usual trail.
Barmen and taxi drivers and friends
all agree he's bad and he needs to go in.
A few new friends reckon he's fine and don't
know what all the fuss is about. I find
a woman in the chip shop who saw him last.
She doesn't want to betray him but he was
saying some dangerous things. I say I know,
not to worry, this is what always happens
and it definitely sounds like he needs to go in.
I tell the community psychiatric nurse and the
doctor again. I leave messages everywhere. Mates
phone me with long drunken tributes to him but then
admit he needs to go in. Another phone call. Now he's
shoving people in pubs. I phone the community
psychiatric nurse, the doctor and the police. Try to
triangulate. I find Da, curled up in front of the fire.
His chasing days are over. That's my job now.
He swears and curses him and is sad. More phone calls.
More doctors and a different community psychiatric
nurse who doesn't know his case. A phone call to say
he's kicked off in his local. I phone the police and the
doctor and another community psychiatric nurse.

He sees me and curses me and pushes me against a wall
and takes my coat. I phone the police and the right community
psychiatric nurse and the doctor and he tells them all to fuck
off. He goes in two days later with a black eye and me and
a taxi driver he trusts. We stop off to buy Diet Coke and
a newspaper. He greets the nurses he recognises and
interrogates the ones he doesn't. There is a scuffle
and he curses me. I go home and wait for his call.

Subway

It was my fault, to be honest.
I'd told him, back when I was a student,
that I figured out if you wanted to sit
and read in a cafe, pick a franchise,
because the staff don't care about profit
and won't notice if you sit there all night
reading a novel or writing one.

So began Francy's lifelong relationship
with Subway. *Meet me in Subway.*
In Belfast or County Down he'd be there,
at the seat nearest the door scanning
the street through the glass front.

I could check things when I was there:
his clothes, his eye contact, how long
he would sit before getting up
for another Diet Coke refill,
how many refills he thought
it was appropriate to get, what
his banter with the staff was like.
I'd search their faces to see
were they enjoying his craic
or if they'd had enough of him.

Maybe it was the maps on the wall
of the New York City Subway
that gave him his bearings.
He'd never been,
but always wanted to go.
Madison Square Gardens, of course,
to fight Tyson or Louis or Dempsey.

It was one of the bad ones, even for Francy,
when he ripped out the computer cables
at his local bank because they couldn't give him
any more money, and he smashed the place up,
threatened the staff, and walked
across the street for a Diet Coke in Subway,
where three policemen tried to restrain him,
an ex-boxer/bouncer who knew all the Jason Bourne
and Bruce Lee movies by heart and was
smack-bang at the peak of psychosis

so when one of the officers was injured
it was all recounted for the court
that found him guilty of assault
based on the CCTV footage
from his local Subway.

So next time he was out,
I was, even for Francy,
a little surprised when he said
that we should meet in Subway.

I hesitated and checked
with the staff out of earshot,
was it OK? And they laughed
Francy? Of course, he's great craic.

So when the outrageous happens,
even for Francy, and he drops dead at 48
on Lower Crescent as the bouncers rush
over and try their best to bring him round,
we can all work out that he's just crossed
Botanic Avenue coming out of Subway.

And at his wake in Burrendale Estate,
sitting there in a fairly traumatised state,
we get a knock on the door and it's
four young women in uniform fleece-tops,
make-up already smudged well before
we show them anywhere near his coffin,
carrying three high-stacked trays of assorted
six-inch baguettes from the local Subway.

iv

Irish for Beginners

i   a haon

Early Irish classes
involved *tch* and *cheac*.
Couldn't get it.

Tá mé was easier: I am.
But the words kept doing things
every time another word pushed
up against them.

And the teacher used to grab us
by the hairs at the side of our ears
and lift us off the ground.

So, at the age of 13 I dropped it,
looking around for another language
that was taught with less torture.

The French teacher was mean too,
but I was better at French
so less likely to get hit.

ii   a dó

Fir, men and *Mná,* women
on the doors of the Croke Park
Stadium toilets, Dublin,
I knew I was over the border.

Tiocfaidh ár lá. Chucky ar la.
Our day will come.
If you said that, you were a *chucky,*
a bit, you know, republican

like the boy from the farm
who used to come to Gaelic football,
pointing his arm as if a rifle
at the army helicopters,
tsk, out of range of boys,
out of range.

iii   *a trí*

Chunky munky.
At St Patrick's Day Mass,
Squinty McLaren,
my fellow altar boy,
whispered in my ear
that the priest had said
chunky munky.

Held in the sniggers
as the head altar boy
was watching us and
chunky munky

he said it again.
We were cracking up now
and I rang the bell
late for communion

and back in the sacristy
me and Squinty had to do
the tunnel of death

crawling through
the altar boys' legs
as they hit us with
their shoes.

iv   *a ceathair*

Seosamh Ó Dubhagáin
My name.
I always liked that.
Dubh. Dark.

v   *a cúig*

Sinn Féin.
In 1970's County Down
that translated as troublemaker,
mad, bad, handles explosives.
Don't be seen speaking to them
or buying *An Phoblacht*
or the next thing you know
you'll be lifted yourself.

vi   a sé

Fir and *Mná* on the
Queen's University Belfast
Students' Union toilets – felt like
someone was looking for trouble.

vii   a seacht

A chip shop in Derry.
Two drunk teenagers
are telling jokes. I strain
but only make out
agus – and
cá bhfuil? – where?

Doire.
Grove of the oak.

viii   a hocht

The *Gaeltacht* man
in the Pac-Man hat
chatting away
about current affairs
in his mother tongue,
odd words in English
alerting my ears
as I sat in the bar
in Gortahork:
motor insurance
and later
Lady Diana.
Talking to his friend
at the bar and
this wasn't a show
or a political rally.

Céad Míle Fáilte,
a hundred thousand welcomes.
First time it really meant anything
was when I was greeted by Patsy Dan,
An Rí, King of Tory Island,
as I stumbled thankfully out of the Atlantic.

On Tory, the Gaelic
rose with the *sean nós* songs
from the tables in the social club
until clunked by a question
in foreign English from myself
or another invader.

Getting served at the bar
I struggled and pretended:
Go raibh maith agat. Thank you.
I am a fluent Irish speaker
but also, a man of few words.

And now the hunger is upon me.
Tá ocras orm.
I learn and use the Irish word for love,
grá. Is tú mo ghrá.
And I scraw and I scratch.

Brian Merriman?
Brian Mac Giolla Meidhre.
There's a whole tribe of poets
waiting to be translated.

His lines fire me
from a depressed January day:

Táim in achrann dhaingean na
mbliadhnta
Ag tarraing go tréan ar laethibh
liathe

I am in the strong grip of years
drawing violently on the grey days.

I buy the book, *A Hidden Ireland*,
and pay a tenner less
off my electricity Easysaver card.
I need this kind of electricity too.

In old-fashioned English,
I read of the Bardic schools,
not just a poem or two
but a tradition,
a nation within a nation,

maybe the nation that
powered the nation.
page 70, *síolta teine,*
seeds of fire.

Ca bhfuil mé anois?
Where am I now?
Tá mé listening.
A fledgling chaffinch
removed from its habitat
can still sing fragments
of its species' song
without ever hearing it,
but needs to hear the
adult bird to
learn the full song.

xi   a haon déag

In the Bardic school
the apprentices
were left in the dark
with a theme to
work apart each by
himself the whole next day
and into the night, till
at a certain hour
lights being brought in,
they committed it to writing.

Facing the dozy fireplace in this
100-year-old Donegal cottage,
I tried this method tonight.

Seemed silly,
but later sprang up
and wrote these pages
you've just read. My
lessons in Irish.

Montague wrote of the tongue grafted
onto us by our landlords as the other
mutters underneath.
When I am tired in England,
sometimes I have to repeat
what I have just said.

Tá an teanga seo i mo chorp
ach chan a thuilleadh ar mo theanga.
My tongue is in my body
but no longer on my tongue.

v

Notes from Oakland

What would happen
if the world ran out of morphine?
My little brother glares at me.
How can I dare write a poem
about this?

Like torture porn with no ad break,
a piranha attack from the inside out,
they still don't show this in the movies,
they still don't show this on reality TV.

I'm following the advice.
I'm being with him.
I'm being present.
And what I see
is a young man
being eaten slowly.

Tonight, I leave him again,
in the care of the Filipino nurses,
and in five weeks at his bedside
I've met more Irish builders and contractors
and electricians and carpenters
and pipe-layers and plumbers and painters
than I ever did in Ireland.

I've joked that I could build a house here
with all these phone numbers
and business cards and coffees and offers
of help and lifts and dinners.
And I guess there is a house here,
the house that Michael built.

No, I mean it,
If you need anything,
ring – day or night.

I have been back and forth
across the Bay Bridge to
Oakland Health Center
in thirty different pick-up trucks
driven by pink-skinned
men and women from
nearly every county in Ireland.

And if they could have,
they would have
built him a rescue contraption,
like MacGyver or the A-Team,
with welding torches and lathes
and paint-tins and concrete and planks.

The Castlewellan Road

After I had been visiting for a while,
got used to his anger,
and realised I was the best person
to receive it,

figured out the last thing
he needed from me
was more fear and discomfort
or banter about football.

Big brother telling his younger brother
he's going to die young and there's
nothing anyone can do about it.

Held his hand for the first time
since he was six and I was twelve
and we had to cross the Castlewellan Road.

Mickey Duggan's Wake

Everyone was in Durty Nelly's
for the party you couldn't make.

There were three clear camps:
your fairly sensible grown-up mates,
your crazy bastard drinking mates,
and your AA mates, some of whom had not
seen the inside of a pub in several years,
but took that risk for you.
Some send-off, boy.

The dollars were getting chucked in the box.
Turned nine times around
and the poor old dog was drowned.

I had six million bottles of Budweiser lined up
in front of me but sure I don't really drink.
I had three hundred guys that wanted to play golf
with me but sure I don't play golf.
I had a woman at the bar that always had a thing
about you and said I looked like you but sure
I am older and taken.

Jesús was there.
Hardly a word of English
but it was him that saved me
when I rushed outside *for air.*

Hair Oil was there.
And a 6ft lad from Belfast
that you'd christened Danny-Two-Beds.
Macken of course. 100 percent.
And I heard the story about the motor bike
and a thousand jokes about Hair Oil's plumbing.
You should have been there.

The Plastic Urn

He got squashed
into that but it's
not a cartoon and
nobody's laughing.

To bring a strapping lad,
my young buck brother,
back to my ma
in a wee lunchbox.
No longer taking up space.
No longer holding his own.
Is this some sort of joke?
WTF am I supposed
to do with this?

This is the part of
the poem where
I normally shift into
a more dignified tone,
remember the good times
and the positive messages
we can take from this.
Turn it around.
But he didn't want
any nice poems.
The look he gave me
near the end.

On Haight-Ashbury, Summer '67
for David Talbot

Beside the Free Clinic
and the busking Donovan double,
the waif from out of state
breaths in her affirmation:

float along this street
between daisy chains
and Robert Crumb fly traps
and you might come down

in the Fillmore strobing out
to Moby Grape, The Doors,
Santana, Otis or The Who,

hooking up with the Diggers,
the Good Earth Commune,
Merry Pranksters, the Cockettes,
or hanging with Janis, Jimi,
Airplane or The Dead.

Someone's blowing bubbles
through the traffic.
They say they're full of LSD.

Break on through and
may your trip be true.
It's only a hippy skip
to the happening in
Golden Gate Park.

There are no spirit signals though,
on how to avoid Jim Jones,
Charlie and his family,
Anton LaVey or The SLA.

Down here, everyone's
talking about love.

vi

Night Football

Francy between concrete bollard goals
because he would dive on tarmac.
I was big bro' in midfield passing it around.
Michael the smallest but had a few good
touches and the odd sneaky tap-in.

Manus and Niall were bigger, with cannonball
shots and hospital tackles. But some nights
we managed to beat them.

We argued and squabbled, me and my brothers,
but we were a team. And when we walked home
after the game, sometimes we'd won,
and we would walk home knowing we'd won.

Only when we left the pitch would we realise
how dark it was. Our eyes had been gradually
getting used to it so we could still follow the ball.
But if anyone walked past they'd ask,
How can you see a thing?

That sensation of playing as it was getting dark.
I can access that. It was getting darker all the time
and we never noticed.

2.40 am

for E.B.

When I was younger I used to do this a lot:
get up in the middle of the night. Come
downstairs. Reclaim the house.

Now it has a pristine feel to it. The surfaces
are bare, the bareness sings with clarity.
The sink and draining board are temple white.

The front room looks incredibly tidy,
like a cleaner left a few seconds ago.
My mind is a moon. No heat. Just reflected light.

Tracking the slope of the armchair.
That chair is an important object.
Placed with intent.

The cooling fan on the TV box ripples into the sea of the room.
Is the buzz just electricity on standby, or the ghosts
of the boys who've gone to bed?

I stroke my forehead and listen to the grazing
of the two sounds: the external roughness of fingers on skin,
and the internal listening of skull. I am intact.

A friend who is responding to treatment talked today
about another friend who is not.
We talked about performing more. Giving it a go.

The Bonus Party
for P.D.

i

In-between hospital visits
I manage to get to my uncle's
90th birthday party
in the little Monaghan village
we'd escape to in the 70's
running away from
the Big Troubles in Belfast
and the wee troubles in my da's head.

Even a few of his peers make it
to hear him clink his teacup
and welcome everyone
to his 31st birthday.

He says if you want to survive
a heart attack at fifty-nine
you have to get organised early
and do three things:
marry a nurse,
live within six miles of a good A&E
and campaign to keep it open.

This, like every party since,
is a bonus party.

ii

I enjoy the party, despite a ferry-lagged
Google diagnosis of throat cancer.
I have been collecting family modes of death
for some time now, and have cancer,
massive stroke and sudden heart attack.
Would greatly prefer the third,
which is why my mind is telling me
I have the one I fear the most.

After a night of panic, I wake up and know
it was a sore throat, plus a bit of stiffness
left over from my walking football.
So I get another day/year/decade/whatever
and all I know for certain is that
I've been let back into the bonus party.

Permanently at Holyhead

Tonight I may appear to be lying
wide awake in this London bed
but I am actually at Holyhead
boarding the ferry to Ireland.

There is part of me,
maybe there is always part of me,
boarding the ferry to Ireland.
Tonight though, I can see the gangway,
feel the cold shock of the sea air,
as I step off the land.

So in the meditation workshop
when the facilitator asks *Are you present?*
I say *Yes*, when I mean *Sort of,*
and when someone asks *Are you happy?*
I say *Yes*, when I mean *Insofar as
that part of me that is here is happy.*

And when someone asks you if you love them
and you say *yes*, you mean *yes*, but insofar as
they are willing at least once a year to cross
the gangway at Holyhead with you and watch
you point at Poolbeg Lighthouse as you enter
Dublin Bay and witness the change in you.

Michael's Fridge

We get there and there's a phone call,
and we're all on the sofa,
and Daddy, who's dead at this point,
says it's from Michael,
who's dead a couple of years.
Daddy isn't that great on phones at the best of times,
and not sure what to do, so passes the phone
along the sofa to me, the oldest brother
who ends up dealing with these kinds of things.
I can see the call is from Michael,
so I'm, like, looking at it for a while
but then think – *It's from Michael!*
Answer it! It's your last chance!
It's a woman's voice
and she wants to talk about the fridge.
She says she is now living in Michael's place
and needs to ask some questions about the fridge door.
I tell her to slam it hard and it will close,
although that doesn't always work.

Acknowledgements and Thanks

Poems or versions of poems have appeared in *Abridged, The Echo Room, South Bank Poetry* and featured in The Attic Arts Club Show *Rescue Contraptions* (2019) with Declan Feenan.

Summer in Belfast and *Look Up, East Sheen* featured on the Fireflies album *Surrounded on all Sides* (Moine Dubh, 2015). *Summer in Belfast* references the poem *Tuscany (1923)* by Vita Sackville West.

Irish for Beginners arose from a commission by the SOAS Endangered Language Documentation Programme, facilitated by Zena Edwards and also references *A Hidden Ireland* by Daniel Corkery (Gill, 1924) and *A Grafted Tongue* by John Montague from his collection *The Rough Field* (Dolmen Press, 1972).

Mickey Duggan's Wake quotes *The Irish Rover* (Traditional). *Haight-Ashbury, Summer '67* is influenced by *The Season of The Witch* by David Talbot (Simon & Schuster, 2012).

Cover image shows Francy Duggan vs. Stephen Kirk, Holy Trinity Boxing Club, Belfast, late 1980's, courtesy of Eamon McAuley.

Many to thank, including: Matthew Caley, Joseph Johnston, Majella Brady, Eamonn Baker, Mary D, Ellen Factor, Danny Brown, Paul Callery, Gill Wing, Francesca & Tim, Stephen & Molly, The Paxton Centre Crew, Cath Drake & group, Nina Walsh, Franck Alba, Dani Cali and the sorely missed Andrew Weatherall.

My deepest thanks to Karen for her support, to Max, Harry and Tommy and to all those who have been there for me, especially in San Fran, Ireland and Crystal Palace.